NATIONAL EDUCATION UNION.

A SERMON

PREACHED IN THE CHURCH OF THE HOLY TRINITY, WINDSOR

ON

SUNDAY, FEBRUARY 16th, 1873,

BY THE

Rev. STEPHEN HAWTREY, M.A.,

𝒦

WARDEN OF ST. MARK'S SCHOOL, WINDSOR, AND LATE ASSISTANT
MASTER AT ETON.

PROV. ii., 3, 4, 5, 6.

OFFICES : 69, CORPORATION STREET, MANCHESTER;
AND
18, PARLIAMENT STREET, WESTMINSTER, S.W.

[No. O 168.]

NATIONAL EDUCATION UNION.

A SERMON

BY THE

REV. STEPHEN HAWTREY, M.A.,

Warden of St. Mark's School, Windsor, and late Assistant Master at Eton.

PROV. ii., 3, 4, 5, 6.

"Yea, if thou criest after knowledge, and liftest up thy voice for understanding; if thou seekest her as silver, and searchest for her as hid treasures; then shalt thou understand the fear of the Lord, and find the knowledge of God. For the Lord giveth wisdom: out of His mouth cometh knowledge and understanding."

I feel that a great responsibility rests on me. For I am going to speak to you on a subject about which men's minds are divided. I shall have to speak to you about the views and acts of those whose opinions differ entirely from my own. It is my wish not to distort or exaggerate in speaking of such views and acts; nor to say anything uncharitable or unsuitable to the place where we are gathered together. You will anticipate that the matter about which I am going to speak is Education—the education of the poor.

The two opposing views in the matter of education that will be brought under discussion in Parliament within a few weeks to come, are :—On the one side, the view of which the text I have chosen may be taken as the summary. My text says that those who cry for knowledge and seek for understanding, and seek aright, as though they were seeking for silver and hid treasure, will find what they are seeking in the fear of the Lord and the knowledge of God, for it is said "It is the Lord that giveth wisdom, out of his mouth cometh understanding and knowledge." In a word, this view is that education cannot be separated from religious culture. The other view is that there are certain things, such as reading, writing, arithmetic, grammar, geography, drawing, &c., which have nothing to say to religion (they call them secular things), and that these can be taught separately from religion, at school. As for the other things, such as truth, honesty, brotherly kindness, obedience to parents, modesty, reverence, the knowledge and fear of God, and trust in Him, and the love of Jesus Christ, they say that the school has nothing to do with these things—they must be taught at home, and by the ministers of religion.

Such are the two distinct views about education. I have tried to state them fairly and impartially. Now I will tell you how the upholders of these views have acted. Those who hold the first view, that secular knowledge and religious culture cannot be divided, have established schools for the poor where the two should go on hand in hand.

And here, let me say distinctly, the Church of England has had a great and peculiar opportunity, and has embraced it. The opportunity I speak of is this: that the whole of our country is divided into parishes, and that in each of these parishes a clergyman lives, generally the father of a family who grow up in the midst of his parishioners. He is, for the most part, on good terms with the squire of the parish and the neighbouring gentry, and (often with their help) he builds schools for the poor in his parish, so that there is hardly a parish in England now where there are not one or more schools for the poor. And the universal rule in all these schools is that it is impossible to separate secular knowledge from religious culture. So the clergyman of the parish goes to the school and begins the work of the day with prayer to their common loving Father Who is in heaven, and the children say with him, "*Our Father, Which art in heaven,*" &c. Also, the clergyman's wife, commonly, and friends—his daughters and sons also, as they grow up—often take an interest in the children; teach them kindly many things about this world and the next which it is desirable they should know; also, they try to make the children happy in various ways, and to fit them for going out into the world, and for doing their duty in the state of life to which they may be called. All this process is carried on year by year, because they hold that religious culture and secular knowledge cannot be separated.

But now let us look at a school in its practical working; and we shall see that it is only in *theory* that the reading, writing, arithmetic, &c., can be separated from religious culture, that in *practice* they cannot. For what would a school become without obedience, truth, brotherly kindness, diligence, &c., and where are the rules about obedience, truth, diligence, to be gathered from? From the Bible which the Secularist would make a forbidden book in the school for the poor. And not only does the Bible direct the children to be subject to those in authority—to obey their parents in the Lord—to be kindly affectioned one to another, in honour preferring one another. Not only does it tell them that their Father in Heaven requires truth in the inward parts—that greater is he that ruleth himself than he that taketh a city, and give them many similar rules of conduct. In addition to this it tells them how to gain the spirit which it inculcates. It says that it is the grace of the Lord Jesus Christ in the heart that enables all to obey, to love, to be pure in heart, to be lowly in mind. It tells them that God their Father loves them, that He showed His love by the greatest gift He could give, and then it says, "If God so loves us, we ought also to love one another."

The vital and fundamental mistake of the Secularists is this, that they proceed, or apparently proceed, on the assumption that children are like puppets in the hand of a performer, which stand, sit, lie, and perform just as *he* makes them; they forget, what you well know, that your children are moral agents; that they have individual characters; have passions and feelings, can obey or disobey; and that a master guides and teaches them best who has hold of their hearts, and brings moral influence to bear on them.

I will, to illustrate this, read to you, from an educational tract which I wrote some years ago, an incident in which I was concerned, when I was an Eton master.

"Not long ago, a boy in school gave way to heedlessness, and very much vexed me by his inattention; we were practising the Psalms for the service of the coming Sunday. I wrote to his tutor to know if he had any objection to my complaining of him; for, by a most salutary rule, we cannot lay a formal complaint before the head or lower master without first conferring with a boy's tutor, and getting his concurrence. The following is the reply which I received from the boy's tutor in answer to my note :—

"'MY DEAR MR. HAWTREY,—I am unwilling that ———— should be complained of, unless you have on other occasions found him troublesome. I have myself been well pleased with him lately. He is one of the best dispositioned boys I have to deal with, his only fault being slowness of learning ; and I have also noticed that he invariably behaves well in church, and is by no means an irreverent boy. Perhaps this report from me may induce you to think that a first offence, if it be a first offence, of this kind in a boy of this character need not be sent to the lower master.

"'Ever yours truly,

"' ————————.'

"When the boy next came to me I took him into a separate room, and told him of the answer I had received from his tutor. As I laid before him his tutor's sentiments, and the grounds on which he did not wish me to complain of him, the emotion he could hardly control—evidenced in his earnest and flushed countenance and suffused eye—told very distinctly the moral power which his tutor had over him. After a few words with him, I said that if ever I saw that he was forgetting himself again, I should look at him, and that would mean :—'Remember your tutor's letter.' The quick and responsive look he gave me assured me that I was within the truth when I added in parting, ' Go along now ; if you keep this in mind it will do you far more good than if I had had you flogged.' "*

You cannot but feel that the moral power which this boy's tutor had over him was of the highest value to him in his intellectual training. And it is hard to know where to look for the source of this moral influence—the influence of human living soul on human living soul—except in those principles, thoughts, feelings, which master and scholar share

---

* "Reminiscences of a French Eton," pp. 11, 12.

in, by the reception of the truths of Christianity
found in the New Testament. I speak not as a
theorist. What I say is the result of an experience
of thirty-six years as an Eton master. And as you
seem interested by the practical illustration I have
introduced, I will give you another.

A friend of mine wrote me a letter, in which
occurred a sentence to the following effect :—" If a
teacher cannot teach a branch of secular knowledge—
say simple equations in algebra—without a reference
to Scripture, I say he is a very bad teacher." In
reply I was able to write to him somewhat as follows :
I have a pupil to whom I am teaching simple equations. We were one day conversing freely together,
and he said to me, " I hate my dame, and I know
he* hates me." He added : " I pulled my harmo-
nium out of my room yesterday, and played it in
the passage, on purpose to make a noise and bully
him. I know he wants to get rid of me ; he has
written to my father. I'll do all I can to spite him."

I knew he was going to be confirmed, and as the
Bible (thanks be to God) is not a forbidden book at
Eton, nor is reference to religious truth forbidden, I
was able to represent to him that this spirit of
insubordination, this ill-will towards the head of his
house, was just one of the things which, in his
promise on the day of his confirmation, he would have
to renounce. I therefore urged him to go to the
gentleman with whom he boarded, and to tell him he
was sorry for having annoyed him, and would not
do it any more, He replied, " But I should not like
to do it." "I know very well," was my answer, "it
is not pleasant to own ourselves in the wrong, but
this kind of self-denial and self-control is exactly the
service which is required of those who are, or who
wish to be, valiant soldiers of the Lord Jesus Christ."
I spoke more to him in the same strain, urging on

---

* The heads of boarding-houses (not being masters) are called dames at
Eton, irrespective of sex.

his conscience scriptural doctrine and scriptural motive. At the end he looked up into my face and said, "I will speak to him." He did so, and altered his conduct towards him. Of course it was with hope and comfort that after this, standing beside him (for one of my duties at Eton was to arrange the boys' places in Chapel on the confirmation day), I saw him kneel before the Bishop to be confirmed by him.

But his self-conquest had another good effect. I observed that he became more punctual and more diligent; he attended better to what I said, and tried to learn more. So that I *was able* to "teach him simple equations" better because I had been able to bring religious truth to bear on his conscience.

Now such incidents as these are of perpetual occurrence if a master is on the look out for them. There are few tutors at Eton whose memory could not supply many and most affecting ones. And I trust I have by these illustrations made it clear to you that religious culture and secular knowledge should go on together hand in hand—in fact, cannot be separated.

The picture I drew just now of the parish school, you will say, is a very favourable one; it is so. All clergymen are not the model parish priest that I described; all clergymen's families are not model sons and daughters; nor are all squires model squires; nor all school masters and mistresses model masters and mistresses. But this I can say:— It was the conviction that the school was not for this life only, but laid the foundation of that religious culture which leads to life eternal, which called these schools into existence. And in these schools the standard, unalterable, to which the parish priest, the schoolmaster, and the children all bow, viz., the Word of God, the Gospel of the Lord Jesus Christ, is always held up and before the eyes of all.

The history of Jesus Christ, His wonderful and most loving discourses, His touching parables, and

His miracles, are ever read, and the mind of Christ
is thus gradually unfolded to the children. The
appeals which His living acts make to every prin-
ciple of love and gratitude in the human breast, are
ever before them to enlighten their understanding
and to purify their hearts. And then all together,
parish priest, schoolmaster, and children, kneel
before the Mercy-seat to ask for help and guidance,
and for forgiveness of sins, negligences, and igno-
rances. In this consists the life of the school.

And now, what has been practically done for the
poor of the land by voluntary agency? I will tell
you. And here I will read from Government re-
turns, which are perfectly trustworthy:—Out of
every 100 schools of the poor in the country, the
Church of England has built and maintains 74; the
Roman Catholics, 6; the Wesleyans, 6; the various
denominations of Dissenters and the Jews, 14; the
Secularists, *none*. It is thus found that the religious
feeling is the only one strong enough to lead men to
build and maintain schools for the poor. And it
must be so.

I see many of the parents of my old St. Mark's
scholars before me. I ask you, Do you think that to
teach your children to read, and write, and cipher,
would have been a motive strong enough to have led
me to devote, for the last thirty years, the time and
means at my disposal to their instruction? No, it
was because I longed and hoped to meet my St.
Mark's boys on the right hand of the great white
throne in the last day, and to see them following the
Lamb in the realms of life eternal, that I sought my
happiness in teaching, loving, and guiding them.

The Secularists, I repeat, have not built or main-
tained one school for the indigent poor, but now they
step in and say, because in some towns and localities
the number of the children of the poor are more than
can be accommodated in existing schools, that school
boards shall be elected, and that these boards shall
erect and maintain schools to be paid for out of the

rates. And undoubtedly where the voluntary efforts of religious denominations have not erected and do not maintain a sufficient number of schools for the poor, it is quite right that it should be done by the State and paid for by the rates.

But here comes in the religious difficulty. We are not all of one way of thinking in matters of religion, and the Secularist says, the way to meet this difficulty is for the Bible to be a closed book in such schools.

It is true that on days and at hours when the school rooms are not required for school purposes, it is proposed to permit the ministers of different denominations, to instruct such children as their parents are willing to send to them, but this is to be wholly independent of the school, and is nothing more than what they are free to do at present, in any suitable locality.

Against such enactments not only has the Church of England protested, but further, a petition bearing the signatures of 800 of the most respected dissenters in the country (though, alas! many of the dissenters have joined the Secularists) has been presented to Parliament protesting against the exclusion of the Bible from the schools of the poor, erected by boards of education. Still, if the enactments stopped here, though the exclusion of the Bible from board schools would be a very sad decision to come to, it might not be considered as unjust. But next month it is to be moved in Parliament that whether there be or not a sufficient number of schools for the poor erected by voluntary efforts, school boards shall nevertheless be elected in every district to erect and maintain schools out of the rates, and that no schools shall be considered schools for the poor but those which are under school boards. And in these schools not only is the Bible to be a closed book in school hours, but further, the schoolmaster is not to be permitted to read or explain it to his scholars out of school hours. And further, it is to be moved that all Government help shall for the future be taken from those schools which for the last fifty and more years have borne the heat and burden of the day. So that henceforth they who hold to the importance and value of Christian education, and the worthlessness of education without religion, will have to maintain their religious schools without any help from the State, and, besides that, will be taxed to pay for the maintenance of these board schools, to the principles of which they are entirely opposed.

These proposed changes we consider to be acts of great injustice. But there is a greater injustice in prospect than even this. It is as follows:—I wish to put it clearly before you. If parents are very poor, and not able to pay for their children's schooling, there is a clause in the Education Act, in pursuance of which the school-pence is to be paid for such children out of the rates. At present, by the Act, the parents are allowed to choose the school to which they shall send their children, even though the school-pence (owing to their great poverty) is paid for them. But a great effort is about to be made to get this altered, and to take away from the parent the liberty to choose the school at which his children shall be taught, if he is too poor to pay himself. The law is to force him, in his hour of poverty, to send his child to school. But he is to be obliged to send his child to a school where the Bible is a closed book, where prayer is not said, where his child will never hear his Saviour's name, nor be told that He is a merciful Redeemer, Who died for him that he might live for ever.

This is that great injustice, that flagrant injury to the poor man, against which our hearts rebel indignantly. In order that you may see the full cruelty of such an enactment I will put it before you embodied in that form, or supposed case, in which it will very frequently occur. A working man sends his children to a Church school, and pays for them out of his wages. It is his comfort to think that

they are taught about their Saviour. The clergyman
in whose school the children are brought up is, we
will suppose, the father's friend and counsellor. The
father is stricken with sickness. His clergyman, as a
matter of course, visits him in his sickness; adminis-
ters to him the consolations of religion, and comforts
him in his dying hour. Who knows not that a
father's thoughts and cares at such an hour mostly
centre in the children he is about to leave; and that
his comfort is often derived from the hope that when
he is gone they will be under the protection and
guidance of one who has been a friend and guide to
himself? The father dies. The widow deprived of
her husband, the bread-winner of the family, sinks
into poverty, and is not able to pay for the children's
schooling. The law nevertheless forces her to send
them to school. And if the alteration is made, that
is sought to be made, (technically, if clause 25 is
repealed) the widowed mother will be deprived of the
liberty of sending her orphaned children to the
school which her husband chose for them; they are
not to be under the guidance of one in whom their
father had confidence—who soothed him in his last
hours. She is to be forced, against her will, to send
them to a school where the Bible is not allowed to
be read, nor is the teacher allowed to speak to the
children of Jesus.

Now this is simply and without exaggeration the
fact, and, therefore, with the concurrence of your
Rector, I invite you to sign a petition which I will
now read. The petition is issued by the National
Education Union. It contains a temperate repre-
sentation of the injury which the proposed altera-
tions in the Act will do to the cause of Religious
Education; and especially prays that the right of
parents to choose their children's school shall be
continued to them unimpaired.

www.ingramcontent.com/pod-product-compliance
Lightning Source LLC
Chambersburg PA
CBHW081456070426

42452CB00042B/2751